TO
MY MOTHER

THE WESSEX LANDSCAPE
OF
RICHARD JEFFERIES

ANTONY CLARE LEES

THE RICHARD JEFFERIES SOCIETY

First published 1990

Published by
The Richard Jefferies Society, Swindon, Wilts.

ISBN 0 9516214 0 8

Printed in Great Britain by
Nimsfeilde Press Limited,
Nympsfield, Glos. GL10 3UA.

CONTENTS

SOURCES OF THE EXTRACTS FROM THE WORKS OF RICHARD JEFFERIES

INTRODUCTION

It is now well over a hundred years since Richard Jefferies left his native Wiltshire to spend the last ten years of his life nearer to London, and yet the landscape of the downland area of North Wiltshire remains peculiarly his own. Edward Thomas in his biography of Jefferies has written: "This country and its people was the subject of half his work, and the background, the source, or the inspiration of all but all the rest." The truth of this must be apparent to anyone familiar with Jefferies' books. After moving to Surbiton he continued to draw on recollections of the area around Coate in books such as *The Gamekeeper at Home, The Amateur Poacher* and *Wildlife in a Southern County*. Then he began to describe his new environment around London and in Sussex but in *"The Story of my Heart"* and his later essays he turned again to Wiltshire and in the most poignant of these, "My Old Village" recollects his birthplace with the peculiar intensity of a dying man who knows that he cannot revisit his old haunts and would not if he could, for fear of shattering an illusion.

Jefferies was born at Coate, a few miles south of Swindon, and spent the first twenty-nine years of his life in the area. The country which was familiar to his stretched from Malmesbury in the North to Marlborough and Savernake Forest in the South, while to the East the vale of the White Horse and the ancient Ridgeway along the downs as far as Uffington were well known to him. As a boy he spent much time on the small farm which belonged to his father and around Coate Water which was adjacent to it. As a young man he became friendly with the gamekeeper nearby at Burderop which gave him access to the woods on the estate and he ranged widely over the Marlborough Downs, the Ridgeway and the forest, sometimes with a gun, sometimes walking twenty miles in a day but always closely observing the natural scene. Farming was not to his taste and he became a reporter on the staff of a local paper and wrote short stories and pieces on local history. Literary recognition did not come until 1872 when The Times published three letters of his discussing the position of the agricultural labourer, which attracted considerable attention. After this he was able to contribute to national magazines on country subjects and have a novel published. Two years later he married Jessie Baden, the daughter of a neighbouring farmer and after living in Swindon for a few years, moved away from Wiltshire while still drawing on his memories of it for his work. Having written some novels, *The Gamekeeper at Home* was published in 1878 and was the first book in which Jefferies showed his true talent as a close observer of the natural scene and sporting life.

There was, however, another side to his solitary nature which had lead him in his youth to escape as often as possible to climb the nearby iron age camp of Liddington to lie in the shelter of the fosse and meditate, as he was later to describe in *The Story of My Heart*. It is here perhaps, and on the downs, that we can come closest to feeling the landscape which permeated his writing. Feeling is the key to his work and it must surely be as a nature poet that he will live on. Some of his essays tend to be catalogues of birds and plants seen and heard on his walks but in the best of his writing, he himself seems to reject such mechanical lists of names and species and strike through to the heightened consciousness which the eye of a mystic can bring to the naturalist.

The photographs in this book have been taken in those parts of North Wiltshire and Berkshire which are still in a real sense Jefferies' country and in Somerset, which he visited later in life and one wonders what he would have thought of the techniques of modern photography. Jefferies lived at a time when it was in its infancy and was clearly fascinated by it. He compared the difficulty of fixing the image on the early photographic plates to his own efforts to hold the image of what he saw in nature for the reader: He himself wrote "When the efforts to photograph began, the difficulty was to fix the scene thrown by the lens upon the plate. There the view appeared perfect to the least of details, worked out by the sun, and made as complete in miniature as that he shone upon in nature. But it faded like the shadows as the summer sun declines. Have you watched them in the fields among the flowers? The deep strong mark of the noonday shadow of a tree such as the pen makes drawn heavily on the paper; gradually it loses its darkness and becomes paler and thinner at the edge as it lengthens and spreads, till shadow and grass mingle together. Image after image faded from the plates, no more to be fixed than the reflection in water of the trees by the shore. Memory, like the sun, paints to me bright pictures of the golden summer time of lotus; I can see them, but how shall I fix them for you? By no process can that be accomplished."[1] In another book he discusses the difficulty of recording the different tones and shades of colour which he found in the open fields and describes how he studied spectrum analysis and experimented with strips of paper each of a different hue to produce a language of colour but this did not satisfy him. Then he considered that paintings too, were incompetent to express the beauty of nature; finally he concludes that neither science nor art can satisfy him in this quest since it is the actual soul of flowers which he seeks.[2]

We can be sure that Jefferies would have appreciated the ability of modern photography to capture and record the scene clearly and in colour but even so, a photograph must always be found lacking to some extent compared to the reality. Perhaps this is because the image is visually too perfect and that magic which only the inner eye can perceive and which requires the use of all the senses, must inevitably be missing in a photograph. Nevertheless, the photographer can aim to strike a cord of recognition within the person viewing the picture or of inspiration to go out and observe nature with a new and more seeing eye.

So much of the countryside about which Jefferies wrote so movingly is still there for those who are prepared to seek it out, and this is what I have attempted to show in photographs illustrating some of his work.

[1] *The Open Air; "Wild Flowers".*
[2] *Field & Hedgerow; "Nature and Books".*

A fir-tree is not a flower, and yet it is associated in my mind with primroses. There was a narrow lane leading into a wood, where I used to go almost every day in the early months of the year and at one corner it was overlooked by three spruce firs. The rugged lane there began to ascend the hill, and I paused a moment to look back. Immediately the high fir-trees guided the eye upwards, and from their tops to the deep azure of the March sky over, but a step from the tree to the heavens. So it has ever been to me, by day or by night, summer or winter, beneath trees the heart feels nearer to that depth of life the far sky means. The rest of spirit found only in beauty, ideal and pure, comes there because the distance seems within touch of thought. To the heaven thought can reach lifted by the strong arms of the oak, carried up by the ascent of the flame-shaped fir. Round the spruce top the blue was deepened, concentrated by the fixed point; the memory of that spot, as it were, of the sky is still fresh – I can see it distinctly – still beautiful and full of meaning. It is painted in bright colour in my mind, colour thrice laid, and indelible; as one passes a shrine and bows the head to the Madonna, so I recall the picture and stoop in spirit to the aspiration it yet arouses. For there is no saint like the sky, sunlight shining from its face.

From: The Open Air

"beneath trees the heart feels nearer to that depth of life the far sky means"
Liddington from Barbury Hill

If we had never before looked upon the earth, but suddenly came to it man or woman grown, set down in the midst of a summer mead, would it not seem to us a radiant vision? The hues, the shapes, the song and life of birds, above all the sunlight, the breath of heaven, resting on it; the mind would be filled with its glory, unable to grasp it, hardly believing that such things could be mere matter and no more. Like a dream of some spirit-land it would appear, scarce fit to be touched lest it should fall to pieces, too beautiful to be long watched lest it should fade away. So it seemed to me as a boy, sweet and new like this each morning; and even now, after the years that have passed, and the lines they have worn in the forehead, the summer mead shines as bright and fresh as when my foot first touched the grass. It has another meaning now; the sunshine and the flowers speak differently, for a heart that has once known sorrow reads behind the page, and sees sadness in joy. But the freshness is still there, the dew washes the colours before dawn. Unconscious happiness in finding wild flowers – unconscious and unquestioning, and therefore unbounded.

I used to stand by the mower and follow the scythe sweeping down thousands of the broad-flowered daisies, the knotted knapweeds, the blue scabious, the yellow rattles, sweeping so close and true that nothing escaped; and yet, although I had seen so many hundreds of each, although I had lifted armfuls day after day, still they were fresh. They never lost their newness, and even now each time I gather a wild flower it feels a new thing.

From: The Open Air

"Unconscious happiness in finding wild flowers"

The soft autumn sunshine, shorn of summer glare, lights up with colour the fern, the fronds of which are yellow and brown, the leaves, the grey grass, and hawthorn sprays already turned. It seems as if the early morning's mists have the power of tinting leaf and fern, for so soon as they commence the green hues begin to disappear. There are swathes of fern yonder, cut down like grass or corn, the harvest of the forest. It will be used for litter and for thatching sheds. The yellow stalks – the stubble – will turn brown and wither through the winter, till the strong spring shoots come up and the anemones flower. Though the sunbeams reach the ground here, half the green glade is in shadow, and for one step that you walk in sunlight ten are in the shade. Thus, partly concealed in full day, the forest always contains a mystery. The idea that there may be something in the dim arches held up by the round columns of the beeches lures the footsteps onwards. Something must have been lately in the circle under the oak where the fern and bushes remain at a distance and wall in a lawn of green. There is nothing on the grass but the upheld leaves that have dropped, no mark of any creature, but this is not decisive; if there are no physical signs, there is a feeling that the shadow is not vacant. In the thickets, perhaps – the shadowy thickets with front of thorn – it has taken refuge and eluded us. Still onward the shadows lead us in vain but pleasant chase.

From: The Open Air

"the forest always contains a mystery."
Savernake Forest

It was a lovely spot, too, for dreaming on a summer's day, reclining on the turf, with the harebells swinging in the faint breeze. The extreme solitude was its charm: no lanes or tracks other than those purely pastoral came near. There were woods on either hand; in the fir plantations the jays chattered unceasingly. The broad landscape stretched out to the illimitable distance, till the power of the eye failed and could trace it no farther. But if the gaze was lifted it looked into blue space – the azure heaven not only overhead, but, as it seemed, all round.

From: The Amateur Poacher

"with the harebells swinging in the faint breeze."

The pale beams of the waning moon still cast a shadow on the cottage, when the labourer rises from his heavy sleep on a winter's morning. Often he huddles on his things and slips his feet into his thick "water-tights" – which are stiff and hard, having been wet over night – by no other light than this. If the household is comparatively well managed, however, he strikes a match, and his "dip" shows at the window. But he generally prefers to save a candle, and clatters down the narrow steep stairs in the semi-darkness, takes a piece of bread and cheese, and steps forth into the sharp air. The cabbages in the garden he notes are covered with white frost, so is the grass in the fields and the footpath is hard under foot. In the furrows is a little ice – white because the water has shrunk from beneath it, leaving it hollow – and on the stile is a crust of rime, cold to the touch, which he brushes off in getting over. Overhead the sky is clear – cloudless but pale – and the stars, though not yet fading, have lost the brilliant glitter of midnight. Then, in all their glory, the idea of their globular shape is easily accepted; but in the morning, just as the dawn is breaking, the absence of glitter conveys the impression of flatness – circular rather than globular. But yonder, over the elms, above the cowpens, the great morning star has risen, shining far brighter, in proportion, than the moon; an intensely clear metallic light – like incandescent silver.

From: Hodge and His Masters

"A Winter's Morning."

Round black marks upon the turf, with grey ashes scattered about and half-consumed sticks show where the gipsies have recently bivouacked, sheltered somewhat at night by the hedges. Nearby is an ancient tumulus, on which grows a small yet obviously aged sycamore tree, stunted by wind and storm, and under it the holes of rabbits – drilling their habitations into the tomb of the unknown warrior. In his day, perhaps, the green track wound through a pathless wood long since cleared. Soon the hedges all but disappear, the ground rises once more, nearing the hills; and here the way widens out – first fifty, then a hundred yards across – green sward dotted with furze and some brake fern, and bunches of tough dry grass. Above on the summit is another ancient camp, and below two more turf-grown tumuli, low and shaped like an inverted bowl. Many more have been ploughed down, doubtless, in the course of the years: sometimes still, as the share drives through the soil there is a sudden jerk, and a scraping sound of iron against stone.

From: Wild Life in a Southern County

"Nearby is an ancient tumulus, on which grows a small yet obviously aged sycamore tree."

A July fly went sideways over the long grass. His wings made a burr about him like a net, beating so fast they wrapped him round with a cloud. Every now and then, as he flew over the trees of grass, a taller one than common stopped him, and there he clung, and then the eye had time to see the scarlet spots – the loveliest colour – on his wings. The wind swung the burnet and loosened his hold, and away he went again over the grasses, and not one jot did he care if they were Poa or Festuca, or Bromus or Hordeum, or any other name. Names were nothing to him; all he had to do was to whirl his scarlet spots about in the brilliant sun, rest when he liked, and go on again. I wonder whether it is a joy to have bright scarlet spots, and to be clad in the purple and gold of life; is the colour felt by the creature that wears it? The rose, restful of a dewy morn before the sunbeams have topped the garden wall, must feel a joy in its own fragrance, and know the exquisite hue of its stained petals. The rose sleeps in its beauty.

The fly whirls his scarlet-spotted wings about and splashes himself with sunlight, like the children on the sands. He thinks not of the grass and sun; he does not heed them at all – and that is why he is so happy – any more than the barefoot children ask why the sea is there, or why it does not quite dry up when it ebbs. He is unconscious; he lives without thinking about living; and if the sunshine were a hundred hours long, still it would not be long enough. No, never enough of sun and sliding shadows that come like a hand over the table to lovingly reach our shoulder, never enough of the grass that smells sweet as a flower, not if we could live years and years equal in number to the tides that have ebbed and flowed counting backwards four years to every day and night, backward still till we found out which came first, the night or the day. The scarlet-dotted fly knows nothing of the names of the grasses that grow here where the sward nears the sea, and thinking of him I have decided not to wilfully seek to learn any more of their names either. My big grass book I have left at home, and the dust is settling on the gold of the binding. I have picked a handful this morning of which I know nothing. I will sit here on the turf and the scarlet-dotted flies shall pass over me, as if I too were but a grass. I will not think, I will be unconscious, I will live.

From: Field and Hedgerow

"there he clung and then the eye had time to see the scarlet spots"

It is a beautiful sheet of water approaching a mile in length, and has so much the appearance of being natural that it is difficult even upon examination to consider it a work of man. The delusion is kept up by the numerous trees, and the romantic scenery around.

From: Jefferies' Land: A History of Swindon

The water was rippling under a light but steady and pleasant summer breeze from the north-west. They pushed out, and while the boat slowly drifted, set the sails. Directly the foresail was up she turned and moved bow first, like a horse led by the bridle. When the mainsail was hoisted she began to turn again towards the wind, so that Bevis, who steered, had to pull the tiller towards him, or in another minute they would have run into the weeds. He kept her straight before the wind till they had got out of the bay where the boats were kept, and into the open water where the wind came stronger. Then he steered up the New Sea, so that the wind blew right across the boat, coming from the right-hand side.

It was a beautiful breeze, just the one they wanted, not too strong, and from the best direction, so that they could sail all the way there and back without trouble, a soldier's wind, out and home again.

From: Bevis: The Story of a Boy

"It is a beautiful sheet of water."
Coate Water

There was a hill to which I used to resort at such periods. The labour of walking three miles to it, all the while gradually ascending, seemed to clear my blood of the heaviness accumulated at home. On a warm summer day the slow continued rise required continual effort, which carried away the sense of oppression. The familiar everyday scene was soon out of sight; I came to other trees, meadows and fields; I began to breathe a new air and to have a fresher aspiration. I restrained my soul till I reached the sward of the hill; psyche, the soul that longed to be loose. I would write psyche always instead of soul to avoid meanings which have become attached to the word soul but it is awkward to do so. Clumsy indeed are all words the moment the wooden stage of commonplace life is left. I restrained psyche, my soul, till I reached and put my foot on the grass at the beginning of the green hill itself. Moving up the sweet short turf, at every step my heart seemed to obtain a wider horizon of feeling; with every inhalation of rich pure air, a deeper desire. The very light of the sun was whiter and more brilliant here. By the time I had reached the summit I had entirely forgotten the petty circumstance and the annoyance of existence. I felt myself, myself.

From: The Story of My Heart

"There was a hill to which I used to resort at such periods."
Liddington Hill

The only spot about the Chace where the wind-anemones grew was in a small detached copse of ash-poles nearly a mile from the great woods. Between the stoles, which were rather far apart, the ground was quite covered in spring with dark-green vegetation, so that it was impossible to walk there without treading down the leaves of bluebells, anemones, and similar woodland plants. But if you wished to see the anemones in their full beauty it was necessary to visit the copse frequently; for if you forgot it, or delayed a fortnight, very likely upon returning you would find that their fleeting loveliness was over. Their slender red stems rise but a few inches, and are surrounded with three leaves; the six white petals of the cup-shaped flower droop a little and have a golden centre. Under the petal is a tinge of purple, which is sometimes faintly visible through it. The leaves are not only three in number, but are each cut deeply thrice; they are hardy, but the flower extremely delicate.

From: Round About a Great Estate

"the anemones in their full beauty."

There is a largeness and freedom here. Broad as the down and free as the wind, the thought can roam high over the narrow roofs in the vale. Nature has affixed no bounds to thought. All the palings, and walls, and crooked fences deep down yonder are artificial. The fetters and traditions, the routine, the dull roundabout which deadens the spirit like the cold moist earth, are the merest nothings. Here it is easy with the physical eye to look over the highest roof. The moment the eye of the mind is filled with the beauty of things natural an equal freedom and width of view come to it. Step aside from the trodden footpath of personal experience, throwing away the petty cynicism born of petty hopes disappointed. Step out upon the broad down beside the green corn, and let its freshness become part of life.

The wind passes, and it bends – let the wind, too, pass over the spirit. From the cloud-shadow it emerges to the sunshine – let the heart come out from the shadow of roofs to the open glow of the sky. High above, the songs of the larks fall as rain – receive it with open hands. Pure is the colour of the green flags, the slender-pointed blades – let the thought be pure as the light that shines through that colour. Broad are the downs and open the aspect – gather the breadth and largeness of view. Never can that view be wide enough and large enough, there will always be room to aim higher. As the air of the hills enriches the blood, so let the presence of these beautiful things enrich the inner sense. One memory of the green corn, fresh beneath the sun and wind, will lift up the heart from the clods.

From: The Open Air

"Step out upon the broad down beside the green corn, and let its freshness become part of life."

Of the broad surface of the golden wheat and its glory I have already spoken, yet these flower-encircled acres, these beautiful fields of peaceful wheat, are the battle-fields of life. For these fertile acres the Romans built their cities and those villas whose mosaics and hypocausts are exposed by the plough, and formed straight roads like the radii of a wheel or the threads of a geometrical spider's web. Thus like the spider the legions from their centre marched direct and quickly conquered. Next, the Saxons, next the monk-slaying Danes, next the Normans in chain-mail – one, two, three heavy blows – came to grasp these golden acres. Dearly the Normans loved them; they gripped them firmly and registered them in 'Domesday Book'. They let not a hide escape them; they gripped also the mills that ground the corn. Do you think such blood would have been shed for barren wastes? No, it was to possess these harvest-laden fields. The wheat-fields are the battle-fields of the world. If not so openly invaded as of old time, the struggle between nations is still one for the ownership or for the control of corn. When Italy became a vineyard and could no more feed the armies, slowly power slipped away and the great empire of Rome split into many pieces. It has long been foreseen that if ever England is occupied with a great war the question of our corn supply, so largely derived from abroad, will become a weighty matter. Happy for us that we have wheat-growing colonies! As persons, each of us, in our voluntary or involuntary struggle for money, is really striving for those little grains of wheat that lie so lightly in the palm of the hand. Corn is coin and coin is corn, and whether it be a labourer in the field, who no sooner receives his weekly wage than he exchanges it for bread, or whether it be the financier in Lombard Street who loans millions, the object is really the same – wheat.

From: Field and Hedgerow

"these beautiful fields of peaceful wheat."

In summer I went out into the fields, and let my soul inspire these thoughts under the trees, standing against the trunk, or looking up through the branches at the sky. If trees could speak, hundreds of them would say that I had these soul-emotions under them. Leaning against the oak's massive trunk, and feeling the rough bark and the lichen at my back, looking southwards over the grassy fields, cowslip-yellow, at the woods on the slope, I thought my desire of deeper soul-life. Or under the green firs, looking upwards, the sky was more deeply blue at their tops; then the brake fern was unrolling, the doves cooing, the thickets astir, the late ash-leaves coming forth. Under the shapely rounded elms, by the hawthorn bushes and hazel, everywhere the same deep desire for the soul-nature; to have from all green things and from the sunlight the inner meaning which was not known to them, that I might be full of light as the woods of the sun's rays. Just to touch the lichened bark of a tree, or the end of a spray projecting over the path as I walked, seemed to repeat the same prayer in me.

From: The Story of My Heart

"the late ash-leaves coming forth."

Out of doors, sometimes in the morning, deep in the valley, over the tree-tops of the forest, there stays a vapour, lit up within by sunlight. A glory hovers over the oaks – a cloud of light hundreds of feet thick, the air made visible by surcharge and heaviness of sunbeams, pressed together till you can see them in themselves and not reflected. The cloud slants down the sloping wood, till in a moment it is gone, and the beams are now focussed in the depth of the narrow valley. The mirror has been tilted, and the glow has shifted; in a moment more it has vanished into space, and the dream has gone from the wood. In the arms of the wind, vast bundles of mist are borne against the hill; they widen and slip, and lengthen, drawing out; the wind works quickly with moist colours ready and a wide brush laying broadly. Colour comes up in the wind; the thin mist disappears, drunk up in the grass and trees, and the air is full of blue behind the vapour. Blue sky at the far horizon – rich deep blue overhead – a dark-brown blue deep yonder in the gorge among the trees. I feel a sense of blue colour as I face the strong breeze; the vibration and blow of its force answer to that hue, the sound of the swinging branches and the rush-rush in the grasss is azure in its note; it is wind-blue, not the night-blue, or heaven-blue, a colour of air. To see the colour of the air it needs great space like this – a vastness of concavity and hollow – an equal caldron of valley and plain under, to the dome of the sky over, for no vessel of earth and sky is too large for the air-colour to fill.

From: Field and Hedgerow

"vast bundles of mist are borne against the hill;"

A barren race they are, the proud poppies, lords of the July field, taking no deep root, but raising up a brilliant blazon of scarlet heraldry out of nothing. They are useless, they are bitter, they are allied to sleep and poison and everlasting night; yet they are forgiven because they are not commonplace. Nothing, no abundance of them, can ever make the poppies commonplace. There is genius in them, the genius of colour, and they are saved. Even when they take the room of the corn we must admire them.

The mighty multitude of nations, the millions and millions of the grass stretching away in intertangled ranks, through pasture and mead from shore to shore, have no kinship with these their lords. The ruler is always a foreigner. From England to China the native born is no king; the poppies are the Normans of the field. One of these on the mound is very beautiful, a width of petal, a clear silkiness of colour three shades higher than the rest – it is almost dark with scarlet. I wish I could do something more than gaze at all this scarlet and gold and crimson and green, something more than see it, not exactly to drink it or inhale it, but in some way to make it part of me that I might live it.

From: Field and Hedgerow

"the proud poppies, lords of the July field,"

Far as the eye can see extends an avenue of beech, passing right through the forest. The tall, smooth trunks rise up to a great height, and then branch overhead, looking like the roof of a Gothic cathedral. The growth is so regular and so perfect that the comparison springs unbidden to the lip, and here, if anywhere, that order of architecture might have taken its inspiration. There is a continuous Gothic arch of green for miles, beneath which one may drive or walk, as in the aisles of a forest abbey. But it is impossible to even mention all the beauties of this place within so short a space. It must suffice to say that the visitor may walk for whole days in this great wood, and never pass the same spot twice. No gates or jealour walls will bar his progress. As the fancy seizes him, so may he wander.

From: The Hills and The Vale

"it is impossible to even mention all the beauties of this place"
Savernake Forest

A little farther and they came to the fosse of the old camp. Bevis went down into the trench, and he and the wind raced round along it as fast as ever they could go, till presently he ran up out of it on the hill, and there was the wagon underneath him, with the load well piled up now. There was the plain, yellow with stubble; the hills beyond it and the blue valley, just the same as he had left it.

As Bevis stood and looked down, the wind caressed him, and said: "Good-bye, darling, I am going yonder, straight across to the blue valley and the blue sky, where they meet; but I shall be back again when you come next time. Now, remember, my dear, to drink me – come up here and drink me."

"Shall you be here?" said Bevis, "are you quite sure you will be here?"

"Yes," said the wind, "I shall be quite certain to be here; I promise you, love, I will never go quite away. Promise me faithfully, too, that you will come up and drink me, and shout and race and be happy."

"I promise," said Bevis, beginning to go down the hill; "good-bye, jolly old Wind."

From: Wood Magic

"they came to the fosse of the old camp."
Barbury Camp

The old house stood by the silent country road, secluded by many a long, long mile, and yet again secluded within the great walls of the garden. Often and often I rambled up to the milestone which stood under an oak, to look at the chipped inscription low down – "To London 79 Miles". So far away, you see, that the very inscription was cut at the foot of the stone, since no one would be likely to want that information. It was half-hidden by docks and nettles, despised and unnoticed. A broad land this seventy-nine miles – how many meadows and cornfields, hedges and woods, in that distance? – wide enough to seclude any house, to hide it, like an acorn in the grass. Those who have lived all their lives in remote places do not feel the remoteness. No one else seemed to be conscious of the breadth that separated the place from the great centre, but it was, perhaps, that consciousness which deepened the solitude to me. It made the silence more still; the shadows of the oaks yet slower in their movement; everything more earnest.

From: The Life of The Fields

"The old house stood by the silent country road"
The Richard Jefferies Museum

MUSEUM

The brown Barle River running over red rocks aslant its course is pushed aside, and races round curving slopes. The first shoot of the rapid is smooth and polished like a gem by the lapidary's art, rounded and smooth as a fragment of torso, and this convex undulation maintains a solid outline. Then the following scoop under is furrowed as if ploughed across, and the ridge of each furrow, where the particles move a little less swiftly than in the hollow of the groove, falls backwards as foam blown from a wave. At the foot of the furrowed decline the current rises over a rock in a broad white sheet – white because as it is dashed to pieces the air mingles with it. After this furious haste the stream does but just overtake those bubbles which have been carried along on another division of the water flowing steadily but straight. Sometimes there are two streams like this between the same banks, sometimes three or even more, each running at a different rate, and each gliding above a floor differently inclined. The surface of each of these streams slopes in a separate direction, and though under the same light, they reflect it at varying angles. The river is animated and alive, rushing here, gliding there, foaming yonder; its separate and yet component parallels striving together, and talking loudly in incomplete sentences. Those rivers that move through midland meads present a broad, calm surface, at the same level from side to side; they flow without sound, and if you stood behind a thick hedge you would not know that a river was near. They dream along the meads, toying with their forget-me-nots, too idle even to make love to their flowers vigorously. The brown Barle enjoys his life, and splashes in the sunshine like boys bathing – like them he is sunburnt and brown. He throws the wanton spray over the ferns that bow and bend as the cool breeze his current brings sways them in the shade. He laughs and talks, and sings louder than the wind in his woods.

From: Field and Hedgerow

"The river is animated and alive,"
The River Barle

To-day, entering the ancient way, eight miles or so from the great earthwork, hitherto the central post of observation, I turn my face once more towards its distant rampart, just visible, showing over the hills a line drawn against the sky. Here, whence I start, is another such camp, with mound and fosse; beyond the one I have more closely described some four miles is still a third, all connected by the same green track running along the ridges of the downs and entirely independent of the roads of modern days. They form a chain of forts on the edge of the downland overlooking the vale. At starting the track is but just distinguishable from the general sward of the hill; the ruts are overgrown with grass – but the tough "tussocky" kind, in which the hares hide, avoids the path, and by its edge marks the way. Soon the ground sinks, and then the cornfields approach, extending on either hand – barley, already bending under the weight of the awn, swaying with every gentle breath of air, stronger oats and wheat, broad squares of swede and turnip and dark-green mangold.

From: Wild Life in a Southern County

"Here, whence I start, is another such camp, with mound and fosse;"
Uffington Camp

"Why don't you hop straight?" said Bevis, presently. "It seems to me that you hop first one side and then the other, and go in such zigzag fashion it will take us hours to reach the brook."

"How very stupid you are," said the grasshopper. "If you go straight of course you can only see just what is under your feet, but if you go first this way and then that, then you see everything. You are nearly as silly as the ants, who never see anything beautiful all their lives. Be sure you have nothing to do with the ants, Bevis; they are a mean, wretched, miserly set, quite contemptible and beneath notice. Now I go everywhere all round the field, and spend my time searching for lovely things; sometimes I find flowers, and sometimes the butterflies come down into the grass and tell me the news, and I am so fond of the sunshine, I sing to it all day long. Tell me, now, is there anything so beautiful as the sunshine and the blue sky, and the green grass, and the velvet and blue and spotted butterflies, and the trees which cast such a pleasant shadow and talk so sweetly, and the brook which is always running? I should like to listen to it for a thousand years."

"I like you," said Bevis; "jump into my hand, and I will carry you." He held his hand out flat, and in a second up sprang the grasshopper, and alighted on his palm, and told him the way to go, and thus they went together merrily.

From: Wood Magic

"'How very stupid you are,' said the grasshopper."

I listened to the sweet-briar wind this morning; but for weeks and weeks the stark black oaks stood straight out of the snow as masts of ships with furled sails frozen and ice-bound in the haven of the deep valley. Each was visible to the foot, set in the white slope, made individual in the wood by the brilliance of the background. Never was such a long winter. For fully two months they stood in the snow in black armour of iron bark unshaken, the front rank of the forest army that would not yield to the northern invader. Snow in broad flakes, snow in semi-flakes, snow raining down in frozen specks, whirling and twisting in fury, ice raining in small shot of frost, howling, sleeting, groaning; the ground like iron, the sky black and faintly yellow – brutal colours of despotism – heaven striking with clenched fist. When at last the general surface cleared, still there remained the trenches and traverses of the enemy, his ramparts drifted high, and his roads marked with snow. The black firs on the ridge stood out against the frozen clouds, still and hard; the slopes of leafless larches seemed withered and brown; the distant plain far down gloomy with the same dull yellowish blackness. At a height of seven hundred feet the air was sharp as a scythe – a rude barbarian giant wind knocking at the walls of the house with a vast club, so that we crept sideways even to the windows to look out upon the world. There was everything to repel – the cold, the frost, the hardness, the snow, dark sky and ground, leaflessness; the very furze chilled and all benumbed. Yet the forest was still beautiful.

From: Field and Hedgerow

"Yet the forest was still beautiful."

In the way of sheer, downright force few effects of machinery are more striking than a steam-ploughing engine dragging the shares across a wide expanse of stiff clay. The huge engines used in our ironclad vessels work with a graceful ease which deceives the eye; the ponderous cranks revolve so smoothly, and shine so brightly with oil and polish, that the mind is apt to underrate the work performed. But these ploughing engines stand out solitary and apart from other machinery, and their shape itself suggests crude force, such force as may have existed in the mastodon or other unwieldy monster of the prehistoric ages. The broad wheels sink into the earth under the pressure; the steam hissing from the escape valves is carried by the breeze through the hawthorn hedge, hiding the red berries with a strange, unwonted cloud; the thick dark brown smoke, rising from the funnel as the stoker casts its food of coal into the fiery mouth of the beast, falls again and floats heavily over the yellow stubble, smothering and driving away the partridges and hares. There is a smell of oil, and cotton-waste, and gas, and steam, and smoke, which overcomes the fresh, sweet odour of the earth and green things after a shower. Stray lumps of coal crush the delicate pimpernel and creeping convolvulus. A shrill, short scream rushes forth and echoes back from an adjacent rick – puff! the fly-wheel revolves, and the drum underneath tightens its hold upon the wire rope. Across yonder a curious, shapeless thing, with a man riding upon it, comes jerking forward, tearing its way through stubble and clay, dragging its iron teeth with sheer strength deep through the solid earth. The thick wire rope stretches and strains as if it would snap and curl up like a tortured snake; the engine pants loudly and quick; the plough now glides forward, now pauses, and, as it were, eats its way through a tougher place, then glides again, and presently there is a pause, and behold the long furrow with the upturned subsoil is completed.

From: The Hills and The Vale

"a steam-ploughing engine dragging the shares across a wide expanse of stiff clay."

FA 1301

Two things can go through the solid oak; the lightning of the clouds that rends the iron timber, the lightning of the spring – the electricity of the sunbeams forcing him to stretch forth and lengthen his arms with joy.

From: The Open Air

"Two things can go through the solid oak."

Following the current downwards, at last the river for awhile flows in quietness, broad and smooth. A trout leaps for a fly with his tail curved in the air, full a foot out of water. Trout watch behind sunken stones, and shoot too and fro as insects droop in their flight and appear about to fall. So clear is the water and so brightly illuminated that the fish are not easily seen – for vision depends on contrast – but in a minute I find a way to discover them by their shadows. The black shadow of a trout is distinct upon the bottom of the river, and guides the eye to the spot; then looking higher in the transparent water, there is the fish. It was curious to see these black shadows darting to and fro as if themselves animated and without bodies, for if the trout darted before being observed the light concealed him in motion. Some of the trout came up from under Torre-steps, a singular structure which here connects the shores of the stream. Every one has seen a row of stepping-stones across a shallow brook; now pile other stones on each of these, forming buttresses, and lay flat stones like unhewn planks from buttress to buttress, and you have the plan of this primitive bridge. It has a megalithic appearance, as if associated with the age of rude stone monuments. They say its origin is doubtful; there can be no doubt of the loveliness of the spot. The Barle comes with his natural rush and fierceness under the unhewn stone planking, then deepens, and there overhanging a black pool – for the shadow was so deep as to be black – grew a large bunch of marsh-marigolds in fullest flower, the broad golden cups almost resting on the black water. The bridge is not intended for wheels, and though it is as firm as the rock, foot passengers have to look at their steps, as the great planks, flecked with lichen at the edges, are not all level. The horned sheep and lambs go over it – where do they not go? Like goats they wander everywhere.

From: Field and Hedgerow

"a singular structure which here connects the shores of the stream."
The River Barle

Coming so suddenly over the hedge into the road close to me, he startled me as if I had been awakened from a dream – I had been thinking it was August, and woke to find it February – for the sulphur butterfly is the February pleasure. Between the dark storms and wintry rains there is a warm sunny interval of a week in February. Away one goes for a walk, and presently there appears a bright yellow spot among the furze, dancing along like a flower let loose. It is a sulphur butterfly, who thus comes before the earliest chiff-chaff – before the watch begins for the first swallow. I call it the February pleasure, as each month has its delight. So associated as this butterfly is with early spring, to see it again after months of leaf and flower – after June and July – with the wheat in shock and the scent of the harvest in the land, is startling. The summer, then, is a dream! It is still winter; but no, here are the trees in leaf, the nuts reddening, the hum of bees, and dry summer dust on the high wiry grass. The sulphur butterfly comes twice; there is a second brood; but there are some facts that are always new and surprising, however well known. I may say again, if only rare, how this butterfly would be prized.

From: The Open Air

"the sulphur butterfly"

All things brown, and yellow, and red, are brought out by the autumn sun; the brown furrows freshly turned where the stubble was yesterday, the brown bark of trees, the brown fallen leaves, the brown stalks of plants; the red haws, the red unripe blackberries, red bryony berries, reddish-yellow fungi; yellow hawkweed, yellow ragwort, yellow hazel-leaves, elms, spots in lime or beech; not a speck of yellow, red, or brown the yellow sunlight does not find out. And these make autumn, with the caw of rooks, the peculiar autumn caw of laziness and full-feeding, the sky blue as March between the great masses of dry cloud floating over, the mist in the distant valleys, the tinkle of traces as the plough turns, and the silence of the woodland birds. The lark calls as he rises from the earth, the swallows still wheeling call as they go over, but the woodland birds are mostly still, and the restless sparrows gone forth in a cloud to the stubble. Dry clouds, because they evidently contain no moisture that will fall as rain here; thick mists, condensed haze only, floating on before the wind. The oaks were not yet yellow, their leaves were half green, half brown; time had begun to invade them, but had not yet indented his full mark.

From: The Open Air

"All things brown, and yellow, and red, are brought out by the autumn sun;"

With the morning star, the light-bringer, once now and then when I saw it, a white-gold ball in the violet-purple sky, or framed about with pale summer vapour floating away as red streaks shot horizontally in the east. A diffused saffron ascended into the luminous upper azure. The disk of the sun rose over the hill, fluctuating with throbs of light; his chest heaved in fervour of brilliance. All the glory of the sunrise filled me with broader and furnace-like vehemence of prayer. That I might have the deepest of soul-life, the deepest of all, deeper far than all this greatness of the visible universe and even of the invisible; that I might have a fullness of soul till now unknown, and utterly beyond my own conception.
In the deepest darkness of the night the same thought rose in my mind as in the bright light of noontide. What is there which I have not used to strengthen the same emotion?

From: The Story of My Heart

"All the glory of the sunrise"

COATE AND THE AREA OF THE MARLBOROUGH DOWNS

Richard Jefferies was born at Coate, a small village outside Swindon in November, 1848 and the farmhouse where he was brought up still survives, with part of it forming the Richard Jefferies Museum. At the present day some imagination is required to visualise the place as it was then. The country lane which passed the farm has become a dual carriageway and across the road from the blue farmyard doors described by Jefferies, where once a stile led into a meadow, there is now a motel complex.

Nevertheless part of the house, garden and outbuildings are preserved and the visitor can recapture much of the atmosphere in the rooms which have been furnished in the Victorian style of Jefferies' day, including the one upstairs occupied by him as a bedroom and study. There is also an interesting collection of some of his manuscripts, first editions and photographs.

Coate Water, a reservoir built to supply a canal, long since derelict, is close by and with its sinuous contours must have had all the charm of a natural lake in the last century with even the canal feeder meandering like a stream. Here Richard and his brother learnt to swim, sail and fish and their adventures have been recorded in *Bevis; The Story of a Boy*. The reservoir passed into the hands of the Swindon Borough Council (now Thamesdown) and is preserved for recreation. The northern end, adjoining Coate has all the usual appendages of a municipal park but the far end is still beautiful, its reedy banks surrounded by trees and an area has been designated as a bird sanctuary. Beyond the reservoir in the hamlet of Hodson Bottom, is the thatched cottage which was occupied by the gamekeeper of the Burderop Estate and is described by Jefferies in *The Gamekeeper at Home*.

Leading off from the corner of the farmhouse at Coate is a lane which passes Day House Farm; this was the home of Jessie Baden whom Jefferies married. In a field on the other side of this lane lies a half buried circle of sarsen stones, to which Jefferies was the first to draw attention. This road leads on to Badbury where is the site of the mill which he described and the brook mentioned in several of his books. It is still possible to trace Jefferies' steps up the coomb to the spring where he loved to drink the pure water scooped up in his hands but to-day the motorway has cut through this area and the spring is dry.

From Swindon a busy road runs through the valley to Marlborough but on either side the fields sweep upwards to the downs which run parallel in two spurs reaching out from the twin camps of Barbury and Liddington. To the south the bluff outline of Martinsell, rising to nine hundred feet, marks the beginning of the Vale of Pewsey. This is fine country for the walker; there is a plentiful choice of routes and the scenery is never dull. The contours of the chalk hills are moulded into an infinite variety of small coombs in to which the wheat fields run up to the steeper slopes like a sea, overlooked by spurs and headlands which jut out into the plain. Ancient tumuli stand out on the crest of the downs and there is a feeling of space and freedom as the eye can wander to the horizon and still see only the hills.

On the west side of the valley Smeathe's Ridge runs out from Barbury and the track along it now forms part of the Long-Distance Footpath down to Ogbourne St. George where it crosses the valley and returns along the far side, passing near to the ancient settlement of Upper Upham. All this country was well known to Jefferies and the exploits of Dickon and his greyhounds, described in *The Amateur Poacher*, took place in this area. The path continues along the old Saxon military way or 'herepath' to rejoin the original route of the Ridgeway on Wanborough Plain. This detour avoids the walker having to use a section which is incorporated into a modern road.

His ancestors had lived at the few scattered houses which formed the hamlet of Draycott Foliatt in the plain below. He writes of this, of the gypsies who used to camp in the old green lane nearby and the down above with its line of trees and the ramparts of Barbury beyond. It is here on Burderop Down that a sarsen stone was erected in 1939 as a joint memorial to Jefferies and Alfred Williams. On one of the two bronze plaques is the following inscription:–

Richard Jefferies
1848 – 1887
It is eternity now. I am in the
midst of it. It is about me in
the sunshine.

Burderop Down and the Memorial Stone to Richard Jefferies

THE RIDGEWAY AND LIDDINGTON HILL

The Berkshire Ridgeway, or simply The Ridgeway as it is usually known, runs along the chalk escarpment which forms one side of The Vale of the White Horse and divides the rolling downland of South Wiltshire from the flat claylands of North Wiltshire.

These two areas form a sharp contrast and gave rise in former times to the expression "as different as chalk from cheese". Up to the end of the nineteenth century the clay country was occupied by pasture, feeding pigs and cattle from whose milk butter and cheese were the principal products. The uplands supported huge flocks of sheep whose close cropping of the grass formed the soft velvet turf of the downland. They were also folded onto the arable land to manure it and enrich the corn crops which were so valuable.

The origins of the Ridgeway are obscure but its great age is undoubted. Animals probably formed the first tracks in prehistoric times as they migrated from one part of the country to another and these would later be used by man. Modern historians have expressed doubts about the view held for many years that all long-distance routes in neolithic times kept to the areas of high land in order to avoid the impenetrable forests and marshes below, but there is ample evidence that the route from Norfolk to the Thames at Goring, now known as the Icknield Way, and then onwards through Berkshire and Wiltshire, has been in constant use for more than 4,000 years. After crossing the Thames it splits into two, the lower route along the valley roughly following the present minor road and originally used in summer, while the upper Ridgeway gave drier passage in the winter. It was along this route that the Saxons are thought to have advanced during the early sixth century, only to be repelled by the mysterious King Arthur leading the Britons who swept down on the Saxons and defeated them at the Battle of Mount Badon to such good effect that the advance was halted for more than forty years. Many consider that the site of this battle was by the Ridgeway, below Liddington.

By Jefferies' day the Ridgeway would have been largely enclosed between thorn hedges and would broadly have taken on the aspect we see to-day. The great flocks of sheep have largely gone but the ancient hedgerows still border the road. Here, at least, no chemical weedkillers or pesticides are used and nature has taken the broad margins back to herself. In summer these are decorated with knapweed, scabious and many other wild flowers, while butterflies flutter between them or rest on the chalk surface of the track. In autumn the hedges are festooned with old man's beard and scarlet hips and haws.

Uffington Castle is a distinctive landmark and it is unlikely that Jefferies would have ventured further east than this during his walks along the Ridgeway. The old track passes just beneath the southern ramparts of this iron age camp and at this point it reaches a height of 850 feet and from here he would have been able to look back along the Ridgeway which he describes as "running like a green riband through the sea of corn" as far as Charlbury Hill and his own favourite, Liddington Camp. On the far side of Uffington the famous White Horse, of uncertain age, clings in its chalk outline to the side of the hill, while a mile back along the track Wayland's Smithy, an impressive long barrow, stands amongst a clump of beech trees in a nearby field.

For the first half of the present century complete peace must have descended on the old road. However, in recent years conflict has come to the Rideway, which is still legally a public road, between those who seek its solitude and the noise and damage to the unmetalled track caused by cars and motor cycles, added to by the local farm traffic. In 1982 those concerned with the problem formed a Society, The Friends of the Ridgeway, which has campaigned actively for restrictions to be placed on vehicular traffic at least at weekends and although the debate continues, their efforts have met with some success.

Where the track crosses modern roads and on White Horse Hill, it can be crowded, particularly at weekends, but between Uffington and Liddington, a distance of nine miles, only one house stands by the Ridgeway and there are long sections where even in high summer one meets only the occasional walker. In such parts one is very aware of the age of this ancient road and of the countless numbers who have passed the same way over the centuries.

Jefferies' shortest route to the Ridgway would have taken him to a point below Liddington Camp where the ancient way has been incorporated for a short distance into a modern metalled road. From here the sprawling mass of the expanding town of Swindon and the motor way which now runs through the valley, predominate. The hill itself looks low and unimpressive. However, unlike Uffington and the other Iron Age forts in this district, no road leads up it and the few who follow Jefferies' footsteps and climb to the top are surprised and amply rewarded.

In *The Story of My Heart* he describes the way in which the three mile walk from his home at Coate and the labour of ascending the hill seemed to clear the blood and carry away any sense of oppression. To-day the clear air, filled with lark's song, can still replenish the spirit and at the top one is in another world. The flat top of the camp is surrounded by a deep fosse and Jefferies writes of one spot on the south-western side where the outer bank had partially slipped, leaving a gap: "There the view was over a broad plain, beautiful with wheat, and enclosed by a perfect amphitheatre of green hills." One can sit in the same spot and look out over the identical vista feeling, as he did, "utterly alone with the sun and the earth". From here both eye and ear are shielded from the changes which have taken place around his old home. Looking out from the hill the view is of nothing but open downland, leading away to the horizon, the outline enhanced by clumps of fine beeches and ancient barrows standing up on the skyline.

Liddington was above all others Richard Jefferies' place of meditation as a young man and the birthplace of the thoughts which he was to set down seventeen years later in his soul-searching book *The Story of My Heart*. He came here at all times of the year, at sunrise and in the heat of the day, escaping from the everyday frustrations of life in the valley below, to lie on the grass-covered ramparts of the old fort or walk in the shelter afforded by its twin banks.

From Liddington one looks across to the other Iron Age fort at Barbury, which is actually intersected by the Ridgeway as it climbs out of the valley. Beyond, the old track runs along the curved ridge of Hackpen Hill and then swings along the downs making for the Sanctuary on Overton Hill, part of the impressive group of ancient sites surrounding the great earthwork and stone circles of Avebury.

SAVERNAKE FOREST

Savernake Forest, lying south-east of Marlborough must have formed the southern-most limit of the country which Jefferies knew intimately. He writes of it in many of his early books and although it was ten miles from his home at Coate, he would often make the journey on foot both ways and spend the day within it.

The forest has a long and interesting history. The first written reference to it appears to be in a charter of King Athelstan made in the year 934 which mentions the woodland called 'Safernoc'; the origin of the name is something of a mystery. John Aubrey writing in the seventeenth century attributed it to the Old English 'sav' (sweet) 'vern' (fern) referring to a species of sweet smelling fern found in the forest and 'ake' (oak): others have derived it from 'savhr' a word for sand or gravel which would be appropriate for the soil of this district.

After the Norman Conquest Savernake was held as a Royal Forest by the Norman kings for their own hunting and by the year 1200 it stretched from East Kennet, some five miles west of Marlborough, to beyond Hungerford in the east and occupied almost one hundred square miles. This area was not necessarily heavily wooded but was a forest in the sense of being reserved for deer and other game and was subject, not to the Common Law but to the harsh Forest Law designed to give maximum protection to the royal preserves.

By the reign of Henry VIII the Forest had descended by inheritance to the Seymour family and it was Jane, a daughter of one of the Seymour wardens, who became Queen of England and in due course the mother of the future Edward VI. King Henry visited Savernake on more than one occasion and Edward Seymour as the King's brother-in-law received rapid advancement; when the King died in 1547 he was appointed Duke of Somerset and Protector of the Realm during the minority of his nephew, the ten year old King. In the same year the Duke became absolute owner of Savernake Forest instead of merely holding it as the King's Warden. An area of forest belonging to a subject is normally known as a 'chase' but Savernake has continued to be known as a forest to this day and in this respect is unique.

It was during the eighteenth century that the foundations of the forest as we know it today were layed down. Until then it had consisted of separate coppices interspersed with open areas; now by the planting of avenues of beech and areas of beech and oak, the forest became continuous. It was these trees planted by the far sighted Wardens of that time which grew to become the magnificent trees which Jefferies must have seen as they approached their prime and many of which we can still enjoy today.

The Forestry Commission took over most of the forest in 1939 on a long lease and during the war the army moved in, putting down metalled roads along the grass rides which are gradually being allowed to return to their former state.

Inevitably conifers have been planted but there are also fine plantations of oak and the beech have been allowed to regenerate naturally. The gap between the planting carried out in the eighteenth century and the beginning of the nineteenth century and that done since the last war is very apparent as more and more of the original beeches are being lost and at the present there are only comparatively young trees to replace them. Sadly too the gales of January 1990 have taken their toll.

In the last century Ferdinand de Lesseps (the builder of the Suez Canal) who must have seen Savernake in the zenith of its beauty, is quoted as saying that it was the finest forest in

Europe. Today that might be considered exaggerated praise but it is still a haven for those, who like Jefferies, love the forest for its tranquility and atmosphere of timeless continuity.

In *The Open Air* Jefferies wrote: "Under the trees the imagination plays unchecked, and calls up the past as if yew bow and broad arrow were still in the hunter's hands. So little is changed since then. The deer are here still. Sit down on the root of this oak (thinly covered with moss) and on the very spot it is quite possible a knight fresh home from the Crusades may have rested and feasted his eyes on the lovely green glades of his own unsurpassed England. The oak was there then, young and strong; it is here now, ancient but sturdy."

Many of the finest oaks have gone, including the famous King and Queen Oaks but there are still plenty of places where one can sit and contemplate scenes containing nothing which would have been out of place a thousand years ago.

EXMOOR

The area of Somerset now covered by the Exmoor National Park was visited by Richard Jefferies in the summer of 1883. He spent several weeks in the district, walking the hills and fishing for trout and although the area was new to him he was clearly fascinated by this wild country and during his short stay steeped himself in its atmosphere and traditions. *Red Deer* was published in the following year as a result of this visit and has established itself as a classic of its kind giving a vivid description of the life of the red deer and the practices of the hunt.

In addition to this book Jefferies wrote several articles based on his exploration around Exmoor and one of them, "Summer in Somerset", published in the year of his death, was later included in *Field and Hedgerow,* a book of essays collected by his widow. This contains fine descriptions of Exmoor, the Quantock Hills and Selworthy Hill with its views across to Dunkery and out to sea; in the beginning however he turns his attention to the River Barle and records the many moods of this beautiful river as it makes its way down from Exmoor towards Dulverton.

All this country remains to be seen very much as Jefferies must have seen it, particularly for those prepared to leave their cars and go on foot.

—ABOUT THE RICHARD JEFFERIES SOCIETY—

By The Hon. Secretary, Cyril Wright

"To afford opportunities for fellowship among admirers of Richard Jefferies; to promote knowledge of his life and works." Over the first forty years of its existence, the Society hs endeavoured to fulfil the aims which were adopted at the inaugural meeting held in Swindon Town Hall on June 30th, 1950, under the Chairmanship of the Mayor. The success of the celebrations in 1948 for the centenary of the birth of Richard Jefferies had inspired Mr. Harold Adams, a native of Swindon to propose the formation of such a society.

Prior to that, the nature-writer had been honoured in the naming of the Jefferies Club at Swindon College, but it had been left to the North Wilts Field and Camera Club and the W.E.A. to organise events aimed to keep the memory of Richard Jefferies alive.

From a small sponsorship of thirty, the infant Society, with an annual subscription of five shillings, grew into a flourishing organisation. The membership in 1921 was 100, and by 1990 – 400, with a mailing-list covering most parts of the United Kingdom and some countries abroad. Among the subscribers are descendants of the Jefferies family, in England and Canada.

The growth and vigour of a society is reflected in its literature. The Annual Report in September and the Spring Newsletter, both printed by offset-litho, and with pictorial covers, had their origins in a duplicated sheet, entitled *Green Leaves*. In addition to these free communications, the Society operates an unusual service to its members of a growing selection of talks and articles at the cost of photo-copying. It also has its own library and research material.

Although the Society is firmly based in Swindon where the writer was born, there are visits to Surrey, London, Somerset and Sussex, where he resided, or which he was acquainted with in the course of his short and restless life. With increased membership the Annual General Meeting now shifts in alternate years to venues which distant members can more easily attend.

The Society's declared interest in, and concern for places associated with Jefferies' life appears in its vigilance and protestations where his countryside is threatened as it was perceived to be when the M4 motorway was planned; when preparations were in hand to erect a petrol-filling station near Coate water; an American Football stadium in the vicinity of the Gamekeeper's Cottage at Hodson, and a development of industrial units and various modern facilities in the Day House area between Jefferies' birthplace and Liddington Hill. Success or failure, these representations have been necessary.

Plaques recording the connection of Richard Jefferies with Surbiton, Sydenham and Eltham; the naming of The Richard Jefferies Bird Sanctuary near Surbiton Station; and the creation of a Memorial Garden in the Broadwater Cemetery near Worthing, for Jefferies and his fellow nature-writer, W. H. Hudson, both of whom are buried there, have received the close support of the Society. Jefferies' grave is cared for by a local member.

The Society was foremost in urging the establishment of a Museum in the writer's birthplace at Coate, which was opened in 1960; and it co-operates with the present owners, The Borough of Thamesdown in its development and in the preservation of the original farm buildings.

We organised the Commemorative Weekend in Swindon in August 1987 for the centenary of Richard Jefferies' death, all the speakers being members of the Society. Two publications appeared at this time in which the Society was involved. A new edition of *Round About a Great Estate*, by Ex Libris Press, with an Introduction by John Fowles, and illustrations by Graham Arnold. Also a symposium with contributions by our members entitled *Richard Jefferies: A Spirit Illumined.* We gave a good deal of background information to the Channel Four team which made the striking film *Man of the Fields,* which was broadcast in the same year, with the voice of Paul Scofield reading from Jefferies' masterpiece *The Story of My Heart.*

In its first forty years, the Society has had but three Presidents. The first was the dedicated Jefferies scholar, collector and editor, Samuel J. Looker. He was followed by Henry Williamson, country writer and novelist, whose writings were strongly influenced by Jefferies. Upon his resignation in 1974, Professor W. J. Keith of Toronto, accepted the post. His book *Richard Jefferies: A Critical Study* has been widely acclaimed. He is the author among other works of a short collection of verse based on Jefferies' writings – *Worshipper of Earth.*

General enquiries should be made to the Hon. Secretary, Cyril Wright, 45 Kemerton Walk, Swindon, Wilts. SN3 2EA. (Tel: 0793-521512) Enquiries about membership to the Membership Secretary, Mrs. Sheila Povey, 20 Farleigh Crescent, Swindon, Wilts. SN3 1JY. (Tel: 0793-535248.)

A SELECT BIBLIOGRAPHY

Many of Jefferies' writings originally appeared in serial form in magazines or as short pieces in periodicals. The following list is not comprehensive but covers his main works. Some were edited after his death by his widow and some by the late Samuel J. Looker who did so much to bring Jefferies' works to a wider public.

The dates given are those of the original publication. Many of these are still available although issued by different publishers.

The Gamekeeper at Home. London: Smith, Elder 1878.

Wild Life in a Southern County. London: Smith, Elder 1879.

The Amateur Poacher. London: Smith, Elder 1879.

Hodge and his Masters. 2 vols. London: Smith, Elder 1880.

Round About a Great Estate. London: Smith, Elder 1880.

Wood Magic: A Fable. 2 vols. London: Cassell 1881.

Bevis: The Story of a Boy. 3 vols. London: Sampson Low 1882.

Nature Near London. London: Chatto & Windus 1883.

The Story of My Heart: My Autobiography. London: Longmans 1883.

Red Deer. London: Longmans 1884.

The Life of the Fields. London: Chatto & Windus 1884.

The Dewy Morn. 2 vols. London: Bentley 1884.

After London; or, Wild England. London: Cassell 1885.

The Open Air. London: Chatto & Windus 1885.

Amaryllis at the Fair. London: Sampson Low 1887.

Field & Hedgerow. London: Longmans 1889.

The Toilers of the Field. London: Longmans 1892.

Jefferies' Land: A History of Swindon and Its Environs. Edited by Grace Toplis. London: Simpkin, Marshall 1896.

The Hills and the Vale. London: Duckworth 1909.

Jefferies' England. Edited by Samuel J. Looker. London: Constable 1937.

The Jefferies Companion. Edited by Samuel J. Looker. London: Phoenix House 1948.

The Old House at Coate, and Other Hitherto Unprinted Essays. Edited by Samuel J. Looker. London: Lutterworth Press 1948.

The Nature Diaries and Note-Books of Richard Jefferies. Edited by Samuel J. Looker. London: Grey Walls Press 1948.

—BIOGRAPHIES OF JEFFERIES AND WORKS OF LITERARY CRITICISM—

Richard Jefferies, His Life and Work, by Edward Thomas. London: Hutchinson 1909.

Richard Jefferies and His Countryside, by Reginald Arkell. London: Herbert Jenkins 1933.

Richard Jefferies, Man of the Fields, by Samuel J. Looker and Crichton Porteous. London: John Baker 1964.

Richard Jefferies: A Critical Study, by W. J. Keith. London: Oxford University Press 1965.

Richard Jefferies: A Modern Appraisal, by Edna Manning. Windsor: Gaby Goldscheider 1984.

Richard Jefferies: A Spirit Illumined. Swindon: The Richard Jefferies Society 1987.

LIST OF ILLUSTRATIONS